After the Rain

The Book of Mitzvah Power
for Adults and Teens

By
Danny Siegel

The Town House Press
Pittsboro, North Carolina

I would like to thank Mark Stadler, Michael Morris, Naomi Eisenberger, Merrill Alpert, students of the Donna Klein Jewish Academy of Boca Raton, FL, and, of course, my Mom (Edythe Siegel, Critic and Proofreader) for their encouragement and help in developing the idea for this book and for offering suggestions to refine the text.

First Printing, 1993
Cover by Fran Schultzberg
Illustration done with the assistance of Debbie Siegel

Copyright 1993 by Danny Siegel.
Printed in the United States of America.
All rights reserved. No portion of this publication may be reproduced without the written permission of the copyright owner.

Library of Congress Catalogue Card Number: 93-60814
International Standard Book Number: 0-940653-35-4

For Ordering Books:
The Town House Press
552 Fearrington Post,
Pittsboro, NC 27312

For Steve Vinocor
Professor of Heartwrighting, T.O.U.
Good Friend and Teacher

TABLE OF CONTENTS

Introduction.	1
Conclusion.	3
The Frammis	4
A Dozen Reasonably Common Things That Need Serious Fixing Around the House	8
Some Things in the World That Are Breaking or Broken And Need Fixing.	13
Tools You Might Want To Use To Fix All Those Broken and Breaking Things In the World That Need Fixing	16
People Who Fix Things	21
The Wright Sisters and Brothers.	27
Two, Three, Four, Five, And Larger Bunches Are Better Than One Person Fixing Alone	29
T.O.U	37
Names and Titles for Yourself If You Want to Make Up A Little Business Card, Some Stationery and a T-Shirt	45
What Began With A Frammis	48
About the Author	49
Other Books by Danny Siegel.	50

Introduction

During the summer of 1991, my good friend, Mark Stadler, and I would wander the streets of Jerusalem and, in a joking mood, would point to something and say, "This is the alleyway of broken dreams" or "This is the falafel stand of broken dreams." We were just goofing off, and by early August, with some earnest efforts, we had developed quite a catalogue: The display window of broken dreams, the taxi of broken dreams, the telephone, the hotel, the notebook, etc. — all of them "of broken dreams".

Months later, the following poem took shape:

The Restaurant of Broken Dreams

It came to seem that
wherever he went
everything was broken.
Even when he chanced upon a place,
it was a matter of most everything in pieces,
the largest thing whole being no bigger than a vase
or a small handbag without a tear or scratch.
As he spoke to people,
he heard there, too, lines like,
"This is the street of broken dreams."
"This is the restaurant of broken dreams."
"There is the car of broken dreams."
And so he set himself to find the best carpenters,
experts in porcelain and ceramics, insulation and leather,
people who knew how to mend garden hoses
as well as surgeons fixed arteries, plumbers.
He learned each trade in turn
and drew each of his teachers into
what came to be known as
The Great Fixing in the Land.
When he died,
bits and splinters had become endangered species,
and little children with glue and tape and nails in their hands
surrounded his bed and promised to carry on his work,
and their parents awoke each morning,
their dreams still whole.

Now comes the book, of its own, page after page flowing smoothly and gently into another form.

As to the concepts:

It comes down to two basic terms related to Tzedakah (Doing the Right Thing) — "Mitzvahs", which I use in its more restricted sense simply to mean "doing good things", and "Tikun Olam", meaning "fixing up the world".

As to the language:

The words came out in the language of children. Now, having finished the text, I suppose it is for two reasons: (1) I have concluded that some things are simple to do. The hard things are, indeed, difficult, but the simple ones should be left as they are — easily done, loaded with impact, and, at times, life-changing. The language reflects that idea. And (2) I wanted adults to read it for themselves and also to share it with children, section by section according to each child's learning rhythms, so they could get an early start applying their gifts to Tikun Olam.

So, this is about simple things people can do to soothe the wounds of the world and ease the ache in the hearts of other human beings. It is about the happiness and joy of doing simple Mitzvahs. Others, who are experts in solving the Big Problems, will write their own books, and, hopefully the combined big and small Tikun Olam efforts that will result will make Life a bit more Menschlich for many people.

Danny Siegel, June, 1993

Conclusion

The Good People everywhere
will teach anyone who wants to know
how to fix all things breaking and broken in this world —
including hearts and dreams —
and along the way we will learn such things as
why we are here
and what we are supposed to be doing
with our hands and minds and souls and our time.
That way, we can hope to find out why
we were given a human heart,
and that way, we can hope to know
the hearts of other human beings
and the heart of the world.

The Frammis

On The Way to the Movies

One day last week,
I hopped in my car and headed down the Beltway
to go to a movie.
It was *Godzilla Comes to Jerusalem*,
the remake of the 1954 classic,
the one where a rabbi had spoken to him heart to heart
about his temperamental outbursts
and unpredictable behavior patterns
and how the rabbi suggested
a trip to Israel on a supervised tour
and how that would help bring him around, no doubt.
No more than a couple of miles out,
my car began running unpredictably
in an outburst of jerks and lurches
that had me very worried.
I was beginning to panic
because it kept going slower and slower,
and because this was the last night
of a limited showing
and if I didn't make it now,
I would never remember the fine details
of the magnificent monster's return
to a decent and constructive lifestyle.

My First Thoughts

All through the car's coughing fit
I found myself muttering to myself,
"The frammis — it's got to be the frammis.
Now where in the world is it?
I'll bet it's slipped off its belt or broken clean through."
And after I had pulled off an exit and on to a side street
and called the Three A's on the car phone,
for the next half-hour until the wrecker came,
I muttered on and on to myself,

"I know where the brakes are,
and the carburetor and the radiator
and the battery and the pistons,
but, for the life of me,
I can't seem to find the frammis,
though I'm sure it's broken
and that's why I'm in this mess
and will never get to see the great lovable lizard
at the Wall or planting a tree
in the Jerusalem Peace Forest
as a symbol of new life and hope."

The Search

While I was waiting
and the sky was turning grayer and grayer
as dusk began to descend over Rockville, MD,
I looked behind the driveshaft
and under the crankshaft
and right beside the universal joint
and in front of the muffler
and even on top of the differential,
but no luck —
it wasn't there.
I *did* know where the rod was
because, when I had just gotten my driver's license,
all my friends had told me,
"Make sure the engine doesn't throw a rod,"
and I was lucky mine never did,
and I recall I had wanted to know where this rod was
so I could make sure it shouldn't be thrown somewhere.
At some point in high school
and with the help of some classmates
who, as far as I can remember,
resembled a gang of your standard street hoods
in black leather jackets and greased-down hair,
I found it,
but they never took the time
to show me the frammis,
though they had mentioned it time and time again
over the years.

I guess it was their way of torturing me
for getting good grades
and always raising my hand first
and making sounds like, "uh, UH!"
(which meant, "Call on me!"
whenever the teacher would ask questions like,
"What battle was the turning point of the War of 1812?"
and,
"If you slice a round Black Forest cake into 12 equal parts,
how many degrees wide is each piece?")
So for the life of me,
I just never could find it,
this frammis the hoods had made up to torment me,
and when this breakdown with my car happened
I was already in my late 40's.
I had never seen one with my own eyes
(as you can well understand),
neither a cracked frammis ,
nor one that had broken clean through,
nor one that had merely slipped off its belt,
nor, for that matter, even one that was working perfectly
and producing a fine-pitched hum up around an F sharp.

The Tow Truck Arrives

That's why, when the tow truck finally arrived,
I was determined to have the mechanic
show me exactly where it was
and how to fix it myself
if I had the right tools and enough time,
so I wouldn't ever miss out again on a movie
or a night out with friends at a baseball game
or cruising the aisles of a grocery store
for an epic cookie.
I really didn't want to be caught on the highway again
with a frammis that's going *ping*
or is knocking against the rings or engine block,
which could cause terrible problems
with everything else under the hood...
far worse than if a rod were thrown from here to there.
Sitting there in the cab of the wrecker with Bubba,

I knew that soon, real soon,
my mechanic would show me
where the frammis was
and what to do if it slips or breaks clean through.
I know she knows where it is,
and just as she knows
how to fix flat tires and leaky radiators
and slippery transmissions and brakes way out of line,
she most certainly knows where the frammis is,
and once she puts her hands on it
and sets her mind to fixing it,
it'll be as good as new,
and with a little patience,
she could teach me everything
so I could fix it myself
if it ever broke or slipped again
on the way to the movies..

The Revelation

All that was running through my mind
or coming out in mutters
at a verbal 120 miles an hour
even though my Dodge couldn't do more than 25,
then 20, then 18, then 10, then one big fat zero MPH.
That's when I started to think about
all those things in the world
that break or break down
or bust with an enormous wham
or grind down with a sorry whine
to a silence that means
Bad news, Mr. Siegel. <u>Very Bad News</u>.
That's where this story began:
with a car that jerked and shimmied,
then crawled,
then croaked.

A Dozen Reasonably Common Things That Need Serious Fixing Around the House

#1

Your Aunt Maxine accidentally catches her foot
on the lamp cord
and pulls out the plug
and everyone winds up sitting in the dark
at dinner —
that's one.

#2

The pipes clog
and when they get clogged
it makes no difference if they are big or small pipes
because whatever it was
that was supposed to go through them
just isn't making it through — two.

#3

Three:
That same lamp cord Aunt Maxine
caught her foot on
manages to develop a short
about a week later
and once again
the whole family is sitting there in the dark
and they have no idea where to find
the glasses on the table so they can take a drink of water
after a bite of unbelievably hot salsa.

#4 and #5

Four and five:
More rain than your neighborhood has seen
in the eighty-three years of recorded rainfall
(or so you hear on the radio)
has come down and washed away some of the shingles
and all night you hear this dripping up in the attic
that is driving you crazy
and you feel like you want to scream,
"Nu! Enough is enough already!"
Five:
the TV has developed a nasty case of
The Insidious Shadows
and at the same time
the videotape gets stuck in the video machine
just when Superman is about to rescue
all the good citizens of Metropolis,
quite possibly from the ravages of
an unreformed Godzilla
before he had experienced
his radical personality change.

#6

For no apparent scientific reason
you get a small hole in the left leg of your jeans,
which interferes severely with
your being both accepted by the "in" crowd
and being honored with the title "universally cool"
at the same time. (Six.)

#7

Seven:
the swivel on your swivel chair
where you sit in classic comfort
while you are catching up on your work
creaks and causes the same reaction in you
as the night of the great rain storm
when the shingles came loose...

After the Rain

even worse because you know there's some oil in the house
but because of Aunt Maxine's poor eyesight
which caused her to accidentally disconnect the lamp
you can't turn on the light
to go looking for the all-purpose oil spray.

#8 and #8, Subsection A

Your unbelievably hairy long-haired dog,
a Great Rhodesian Harrier Hound,
(with pedigree papers all the way back to
great-great-great grandparents,
champions, every one of them)
has decided to shed on your favorite blanket...
no one else's. Yours.
That's eight.
(Number Eight, Sub-section A:
The additionally terrible news
that on the very same day, Latke,
your Great Rhodesian Harrier Hound
decided to chase Kugel,
your many-colored-but-sometimes-ornery-
and-definitely-overweight cat,
all over the house,
resulting in
(1) an overturned vase of absolutely gorgeous flowers
the family bought to brighten up the dining room,
the vase now lying in anywhere from 27 to 108 pieces on the rug,
in a pool of water staining that same fabulous rug
(2) an extensive number of scratched and ripped curtains,
(3) a bag of groceries
(including 3 bags of potato chips
and a jumbo-sized box of Product 19
now scattered and shredded all over the kitchen table,
a definitely psychotic, though quite natural, acting out
on the part of the terrified cat,
and (4) 16 formerly-neatly-piled comic books on the desk
similarly shredded and scattered
over an area approximately the size
of a medium-sized football stadium.

#9

Nine:
the toaster demonstrated
a tad too much sensitivity
to the grids on the last instant waffles
you had in the freezer
and tossed them through the open window
(it was mid-Springtime
and the windows were open
so everyone could enjoy the wonderful smell of the flowers)
out into the back yard
where two very athletic squirrels grabbed them
and merrily carried them up a 35-foot maple.
How merry they were was demonstrated
by how fast they were wagging their tails
and, perhaps, that faint cynical smile
any bystander could see on their cute little faces.

#10

Your stapler was out of staples —
this is #10 —
and no one else had any in the house
(which happens, on average, only about once every four years)
and you decide to risk it
and carry your book review to class unstapled
but, sad to say, you accidentally trip on a rock
and just then a breeze comes up out of nowhere
and all 13 pages go flying in all directions
and much higher even than the branch
whereon the squirrels of #9 sat snarfing your waffles,
and you just know that
if all the papers had been stapled together,
the report (on the tricky topic of
"How Much Hebrew Did Shakespeare Really Know?")
would have been too heavy for any wind to carry away,
except maybe a hurricane
which never comes to Kenosha, Wisconsin, anyway,
and you know you are going to have a really hard time
explaining this one to the teacher.

#11

Eleven:
Dad — thinking it was open —
backs the car right into the garage door.
(He was wrong,
and he has had to waste the better part of a day
thumbing through all kinds of ancient texts
to see if there is a prayer for insurance coverage.)

#12

And Twelve:
on an incredibly sunny day
with 9 friends waiting on the court down the block,
your basketball is discovered to be
(to put it very gently) flat.
Very flat.
And, of course, there's really no need to mention
that no one in the house has a needle or pump.

#13-15 Out of 12

That's an even dozen,
though if you want a baker's dozen,
you can throw in
a rusty blade on your ice skates
or your bicycle seat viciously chewed through by the gerbil
your friend asked you to watch for her
while she went on vacation with her family,
or, if you are so moved,
the chocolate chip and walnut cookies
you are still scraping off the sides of the oven
after three full hours
because you put in much too much baking powder
and they exploded all over the place.

After the Rain

Some Things in the World That Are Breaking or Broken And Need Fixing

The World Breaking and Broken

When a flood comes rushing through a town
and soaks people's basements
and ruins their furniture,
and some of the people are left without homes
because the whole house floated away,
we say that part of the world is broken.
And when hundreds of people get together
to help dry out the damaged houses
and take in the families that lost their homes
and then start to work with them to build new houses
we say they have done some Tikun Olam, World-Fixing.
The world is broken in a very big way
when there are wars.
Making peace is Tikun Olam, World-Fixing.
If you have met or read about or heard about or seen on TV
children who don't have any toys or stuffed animals
or games or books
or are hungry,
then, too, the world is definitely broken,
and if you start a food drive or toy drive
or stuffed animal and game and book drive
(making sure to include some of your own food
or stuffed animals or other toys or books),
you are doing a lot of Tikun Olam.
You are repairing that part of the broken world.
You may have even noticed that some restaurants
are throwing out a lot of perfectly good food
just a few blocks away from
where there are hungry people.
If you decide to talk to
the manager and owner of the restaurant
and work with them

to get the good, tasty food to the hungry people,
you have done a lot of Tikun Olam.
By the time you are finished,
the world won't be quite so broken.
And the same is true if you see a place
that doesn't have a ramp
and you say to yourself,
"How can someone who uses a wheelchair
enjoy coming to this place if there is no ramp?"
and then you go out
and make all the arrangements to put in a ramp,
one less broken part of the world will be broken.
The world needs to be repaired
just as much as a broken plate needs to be repaired,
or a computer screen that goes totally blank
for no reason you can figure out.
Giving away some of your clothes
to people who need them
certainly is one of the millions of ways
to fix up the world.
There's no doubt about it.
The same goes for doing everything you can
to scrub the sky clean
because it has too much dirt and carbon monoxide
and other harmful things in it
like all those chemicals that make acid rain,
to be perfectly blue on a clear day in mid-July,
besides all the streams and rivers and lakes and oceans
that need to be made fresh and pure again
and the ground, too,
which needs a good cleaning because of toxic wastes.
All of that clean-up is Tikun Olam.
And something like planting trees is another,
a really simple way to do it,
all the way up to people who donate their bone marrow
to someone who needs it,
which is a little more complicated,
though it is not very painful.
As I said,
there are millions of ways to fix up the world.

Hearts Breaking and Broken

Besides,
sometimes, if people are sad,
we say they have a broken heart.
We can fix those, too.
Sometimes all it takes is to sit there and listen
and be a friend.
They may be lonely,
and if you come along and be a good friend,
their loneliness will disappear.
That is a good way to fix a broken heart.
There are many times we can think of people
whose heart needs to be repaired
if we would only sit down and think about it.
Sometimes fixing broken or breaking hearts is hard to do,
and sometimes it is as easy as planting a tree
or changing a light bulb or plugging in a toaster or TV.
We just have to look around for those broken hearts
and say to ourselves, "Let's do it!"
and then we do it.
And then their hearts will work just fine,
just like my Dodge worked just fine
after my mechanic had finished her work.

Tools You Might Want To Use To Fix All Those Broken and Breaking Things In the World That Need Fixing

A Very Long List

There are so many kinds of tools people use
to fix things up,
I can't even make a complete list.
I don't think I could even name
all the categories of tools,
the instruments and implements and apparatuses
contraptions, widgets, gadgets and gizmos
and thingies and whatchamacallits and thingamabobs
we can't remember the names of sometimes.
It would take pages and pages,
or, more likely, a shelf of books just to name them.
There are so many of them,
I doubt anyone could say them all in one breath —
even my short list of them —
though a good diver might do it
if he or she practiced holding his or her breath a long time
and you are welcome to try if you want to,
though I would suggest you try
one breath for every bunch of few lines.

Clippers and Scissors Small, Medium, and Large

There's
clippers and scissors,
small, medium and large,
and shears if you have to prune your rose bushes,
and pinking shears if you have to make zigzags
when you want to make a new dress,
paint and ink and brushes and pens and magic markers
by the trunkload and carload
and vanload and truckload and railroadcarload,

scales, rulers, protractors and compasses,
calipers, T-squares and triangles,
regular old hammers carpenters call clawhammers,
the ones with the big claw
to pull nails that didn't go in straight out of a board,
jackhammers and sledgehammers
and hammers called ball peen hammers,
screws and washers,
and nails that are weighed and sold by the pennyweight,
chisels, and saws, awls,
pulleys and winches, monkey wrenches,
right- and left-handed ratchets,
needles and thread, pumps and brushes,
zippers and Velcro and clasps
scoops,
pincers, tweezers and tongs, drills;
planes, trowels,
ribbons and tape (wide and narrow, thick and thin),
glue that sometimes works and sometimes doesn't
and paste that pastes things together just for today
and paste that pastes tight for a year or forever.

And Things That Measure Other Things

And there's
an unbelievable variety of gauges and meters
such as:
rain gauges and depth gauges,
wind gauges some people named "anemometers",
barometers and thermometers,
voltmeters, ohmmeters, and lightmeters,
(though I have often wondered
if there is such a thing as a "darkmeter",
and once I even couldn't sleep
because I was thinking about it),
hydrometers and hygrometers,
odometers, speedometers, tachometers
and sphygmomanometers
that measure your blood pressure,
though it's so hard to pronounce the word
you are allowed just to say "sphyg" like the doctors do,

altimeters, pedometers
and measures that measure kiloliters and millimicrons
and those impossible-to-see things that are only
an Angstrom or two long
or weigh only five or six billionths of an ounce
and maybe even a furlong-counting machine,
or if you feel an urge to know
how many light-years away the Milky Way is
on any particular night you are out looking at the stars
so you can set your watch exactly
without a doubt you will need your telescope
and light-year tape measure
in tip-top working order
to set your watch exactly.

Woofers and Tweeters

And there's
three or four styles of keyboards
on microwave ovens that tell you
which button defrosts and which reheats;
[you may take a breath now if you think you have to],
a bunch of charts, a set of blueprints,
a collection of rasps and files of every size
(*very, very* important),
levers and levels, cranks and cranes and derricks,
plumb bobs, scopes: gyro and peri and micro,
and other goodies that doctors and nurses use every day
depending on what part of the body
they are fixing up at the moment,
like Band-aids and casts, EKG's and EEG's, scalpels,
CAT scans for people
(which always made me wonder if they used
PEOPLE scans for cats, but I never found out),
and (*very, very* useful at certain times) a hemostat or two;
typewriters and xerox machines,
computers and printers, modems and faxes,
maybe (but I'm not sure)
things called woofers and tweeters,
though I don't really know what they do
or if they really are tools at all.

Take Another Deep Breath

There's:
shovels and picks,
rakes and hoes,
sickles and scythes,
bulldozers, tractors, and dumptrucks,
cranes, and forklifts for the Big-Time Stuff,
pitchforks — ah, yes, pitchforks
and anything-else-with-three-or-four-good-sized-prongs,
because say there's all this hay out in someone's fields
and all of a sudden the farmer gets sick
and he or she can't pile it high on the truck
to bring it safely into the barn before it goes bad,
so you would certainly need a bunch of haylifters
to lift the hay
and you most certainly would need a pitchfork or two
or anything-else-with-three-or-four-good-sized-prongs,
and where in the world would you be
if there were all kinds of little things
scattered around the yard of someone
who couldn't clean up the yard all by himself or herself
and you really, really wanted to see the yard all clean....
among all the other things
you would need would most certainly be
anything-else-with-three-or-four-good-sized-prongs
which you would probably pick up at a store
that sells
anything-else-with-three-or-four-good-sized-prongs.
I mean,
where would you be without
something that looks like a prong?
And what would this yard look like
if there weren't prongs in this world
and people to use the prongs
to make a yard look just right?
I mean, really,
everyone should have at least at least one
something-with-three-or-four-good-sized-prongs
in the garage.

What the Tools Are For, Anyway

And now comes the big question:
What can you do with all these tools
besides what you usually do with them?
You can take your human tools —
your mind, your heart, your soul, and your body,
those faces, eyes, ears, hands, arms, and feet —
and think of ways to use them for Mitzvahs.
Along the way,
I am sure you will need to use
some T-squares and voltmeters
and cranes and awls and paints
(you *always* need blue paint for Mitzvahs),
because, really,
all these tools are just tools
just sitting there
waiting for you to use them for Mitzvahs.
That's what Tikun Olam is all about,
and that is how you fix up the world
and all the hearts in the world
that need a little or a lot of fixing up.

People Who Fix Things

The Makers and The Smiths

Well, of course,
there's shoemakers and sandalmakers and candlemakers
who can do a fine job of straightening up a candle
that's leaning too far over to one side to be safe,
and blacksmiths and goldsmiths and silversmiths
and tinsmiths, coppersmiths and coopersmiths
(they do barrels; the best for fifty miles around;
if you have a badly bent barrel
lying around the living room,
it would be best to look up "coopersmith"
in the Yellow Pages;
they have also been known to do astonishing work
on sadly warped casks
and tubs corroding away to nothing).

A Variety of Other Fixers

There's:
plumbers and electricians...they fix things,
and car mechanics,
and all those other people who take care of machines
like dishwasher repairpersons
and washing machine repairpersons
and airconditioning repairpersons.
I even know people who repair electric wheelchairs
and because electric wheelchairs are so heavy
and can't fold up and be put in a trunk
like regular wheelchairs,
they have a mobile electric wheelchair repair shop
that comes to your house to fix it.
Drycleaners are certainly the best people around
to get the stains out of a shirt.
They are experts at figuring out
what stain remover works best against
which kind of grease or oil

or a piece of blueberry pie that bounced off your shirt
on down to your tie, down to your pants.
and finally down to the carpet.
Bookbinders do great fixing-up, too,
glueing pages back into books
and fixing the binding so it is good as new.
Watchmakers:
an excellent choice if your watch runs slow or fast
or just gave up one day and died on you at 11:03 a.m.
just when you needed it to time a speech
or a 100-yard dash or mini-marathon.
There's even a few people in the world
who know how to restore great paintings
that might have been damaged in a fire
or who can fix up priceless violins
that someone carelessly left in a damp place too long
and now sounds a little bit off key,
thereby throwing the entire orchestra into an uproar.

Especially the Gardeners

Ah, gardeners:
they can take a back yard that looks like a jungle
and plant and replant and re-arrange and trim
and choose one kind of a tree instead of another
or this bush instead of that shrub
and Wow!
in April, the jungle is now bursting with colors
and beautiful combinations of blossoms and blooms
that make it a pleasure to sit out back
and read a book or just do nothing in particular
but look at the beautiful colors.
They *really* know how to fix things.
Where I come from
we even have someone on the radio
who knows everything about plants and trees and flowers
and can tell you exactly what to do
if your azaleas have developed
a serious case of the Creeping Crud
or your pear tree has come down
with Third Degree Galloping Rot.

He'll say something like,
"Now, on March 16th at 2:00 p.m.,
replant the azaleas exactly 13.4 feet to the left
where there's more shade
and add a pint and three quarters of water
every 19 minutes for 3 days in a row."
Or,
"Draw a green line 4 inches wide
1/3 of the way up the trunk of that pear tree
and stay up all night on the next full moon
and, if you don't hear any wolves howling
where you live in the Washington suburbs,
your pears will be all right."
He *really* knows how to fix things.

And Particularly the Veterinarians

And just think of veterinarians
and how good they are at fixing things.
Some of them can cure
any bird or fish of allergies
or sew up your cat's ear if it got into a fight
and came out on the short end
or if Raizel, your Miniature Rhodesian Harrier Hound,
has lost her appetite,
they'll know exactly what treatment will get her
(The Miniature Rhodesian Harrier Hound)
to bounce back to a full and nutritious diet
so she can go right back down to her real job,
namely, shedding all over the house.
They're the best with pets,
and some even specialize in strange ones
like if your boa constrictor is bent all out of shape,
they can unbend them,
or if you happen to have an iguana
that is mysteriously turning a pale orange,
and is acting more sluggish than normal
they know exactly what to add to the iguana food
to get them back to a healthy green
and have them back hopping frantically on all fours
as is appropriate to their species.

And then there are the vets who are just super
with farm animals
who can help a sheep get over a bad cold or the flu
or a horse that's having a tough pregnancy
that ends up with a smooth-as-silk delivery,
and delivers a gorgeous, wobbly-legged shiny new colt,
which you will want to name "Bracha"
because it is such a blessing,
this birth of a new colt,
or maybe "Nes"
because birth in general
and birth of a magnificent colt in particular
is such a major miracle.
My favorites, though, are the ones that work
in the jungles and rain forests or zoos.
They are so good at what they do
they know exactly how to handle
a tiger with laryngitis
or a flamingo with a molar growing at the wrong angle
or an owl with cataracts that keeps missing its perch
or even —
I heard about this from a friend —
how to get a crick out of a giraffe's neck,
a very serious problem for a giraffe,
you must admit.

The Scientists

And we can't forget the archeologists
who can piece together bits and pieces
of ancient pottery
and then tell us all about the ancient people
who lived on the land
and what they did right
and what they did wrong
so we'll know better how to live right.
And we certainly can't forget the paleontologists
who might find all kinds of brontosaurus bones
lying around and can put them together
like a humongous jigsaw puzzle
into one huge skeleton

so they can tell us what went right back then
and what went wrong back then
and why the the brontosauruses and tyrannosauruses
and stegosauruses and triceratopses disappeared
and what we should do to make sure
that we don't do the same and disappear.
And we shouldn't forget, either, the entomologists
who know everything there is to know about bugs
and can tell us how many earthworms per acre
is a safe number
and how many is too many
and not good for the potatoes or soybeans
we are trying to grow.
And we wouldn't want to forget the ornithologists either,
who know terns and black-chinned sparrows
and great crested flycatchers and lesser prairie chickens
and red-shouldered and zone-tailed and rough-legged hawks
and peregrine falcons and kestrels and merlins
(to say nothing of anhingas and grebes)
and can tell us
if something we did interrupted their flight patterns
or if we are accidentally upsetting their nesting habits,
things we wouldn't want to do.

To Be An Expert

We just wouldn't know what to do about those birds,
or, for that matter, the tie with the blueberries on it,
or our knotted-up boa constrictor
without all these people who are the best of the best
in fixing things
which is why it wouldn't hurt
if everyday people starting to think about
what they are best at
when it comes to fixing things.
There are so many things to be fixed,
everyone can do something,
even if he or she doesn't know exactly
the right kind of tea
that will get a tiger's voice back to full and glorious roar
or hasn't figured out how to

get a crick out of a giraffe's neck
so it can get back to doing what it does best,
namely, looking beautiful
and scanning the far stretches of the jungle
for dangers the shorter animals wouldn't know about
if it didn't warn them.

The Wright Sisters and Brothers

Introducing The Wright Family

In the old days,
once upon a time a long time back,
there were people called wheelwrights
who used to make and repair wheels.
Years and years ago,
there were people who made a living as cartwrights.
They used to make and repair carts.
Once upon a time in the old days,
there were even wainwrights.
Their job was to build wagons and fix them up
if they broke down,
like if their spokes got bent
when they went over a big rock,
and shipwrights,
well, you can guess....
they were good at building and fixing ships
if the rudder or a boom got all warped
or if a mast broke or the sails got ripped in a big storm
(which is definitely not a good thing to happen
to a boat or ship
if it has to get from here to there
to deliver its cargo
of cheese or flanges or grapefruits or orange-colored flags
or take its passengers on a vacation to the Bahamas)...
If boat things broke,
shipwrights were definitely the ones to call over to the dock
to make everything shipshape again.

The Union

What we really need now
are lots and lots of heartwrights
and bunches of worldwrights
and maybe when they got together,
they could call themselves

After the Rain

The International Sisterhood and Brotherhood
of Heartwrights and Worldwrights,
who are great experts
in repairing hearts that are bruised or worn down
or breaking or already broken,
and The Greatest Living Authorities
in building up and rebuilding parts of the world
that have fallen apart
and desperately need to be put back together just right.
Or maybe they could just call themselves
The Wright Sisters and Brothers.
Yes, we could definitely use
groups and teams and bunches of people like that,
maybe even schools of them and flocks of them
and droves and herds
and at least one or two mighty multitudes of them
to do the job.

Much-Needed New Measuring Devices

And while they are at it,
if they have some spare time,
it would help
if some of the Heartwrights and Worldwrights
invented a kindmeter and sweetmeter,
so we could get a better idea
how much kindness and sweetness it takes
to do certain kinds of Tikun Olam the best way possible.
Oh, and a pleasantness and gentleness and niceness gauge
wouldn't hurt either,
if they have time to get down to it.

Two, Three, Four, Five, And Larger Bunches Are Better Than One Person Fixing Alone

The "Re" words

With a little research by my friends
who reviewed many pages in the dictionary,
we came up with a list of Tikun Olam words
that describe many ways
to get down to repairing just right.
Tikun Olamniks can do any one of these,
and a bunch of them together...well,
you can just imagine how much they can get done.
They can:
redo, recondition, recompile,
refigure and reconfigure,
reconnect, recopy,
redraft, redrill, reenergize, reequip,
reface and refence,
refurbish, regrind, regroove, and rehinge.
Or they could:
reinstall, reknit, relacquer, relandscape, relight, relink,
remeasure, remix, remodel,
remold, renail, or reoil.
Or they might want to:
repave, repolish, reroof, rerepeat,
resew, resow, or reseal.
Or, if they prefer,
there's always the possibility they could
reshingle, restack, restart, restock, restuff, retie, or retune.
(Say a person needs to hold on to a job;
say it all depends on the car,
but the car breaks down.
Most of all what is needed right then, right there,
is a fabulous retuner.
And if you look at the last line in this list

you'll see that a realigner
could take a look at the wheels
while the car is in the garage
and could realign them
if the realigner thinks it would make a difference, too.)
They could also:
retype, reupholster,
rewarm, reweave, rewire, rewrap,
rewrite and rerewrite
and, I forgot way at the top — realign.

The International Sisterhood and Brotherhood of Heartwrights and Worldwrights, Also Known As The Wright Sisters and Brothers, Tikun Olamniks Every One of Them, Put the "Re" words to Work

The International Sisterhood and Brotherhood
of Heartwrights and Worldwrights
would no doubt put in their newsletter
some kind of article about how
it is wonderful for every person
to go around reoiling and reconnecting
all those things that need to be reoiled and reconnected
for the sake of Tikun Olam,
but the article would go on and say that
two people together would do that much more
and three sometimes even better than two
and groups small, mid-size,
and too many for the eye to see would be,
in some cases, even better than a mid-size bunch.
Just think for a minute about all the doors
that need to be rehinged,
including doors where people live
who don't have enough money for both
food for the month
and a rehinger to come in to fix the door,
so they choose the food because they *have* *to* have food,
and the door hangs loose, nearly off its hinges,

and the cold wind comes howling in in December,
and the children get colds and the flu
and give the colds and flu to their parents
and their parents can't go to work
and everything gets worse and worse
and then there's not even enough money for food.
If one rehinger goes around rehinging,
how many doors can he or she rehinge
in a day or a week or a month?
Wouldn't it be better if there were
2 or 3 of them
or 10 or 20 of them
and they could cover a whole neighborhood
or small town in a few days?
And if they brought with them their friends
the rewirers and reshinglers for the roof
and refencers for the fence
whose slats are leaning and peeling
and have holes all over them,
and the renailers and redrillers
and resodderers and reconnecters
who could just cover the house from top to bottom
until it was like new,
including the resodders and a relandscaper
who could give the back lawn
a good once-over
so it would be a nice, pleasant place
to sit with the family
so they could think about ways they could also do
all kinds of Tikun Olam.
This crew of Repeople could do quite an impressive job
in just a few short hours or a day or two.

Three of the Heartwrights,
Ilana, Reena, and Shosh,
Make the Rounds
With Their Portable Stereo Tape Deck

Ilana, Reena, and Shosh Heartwright
made it their business to look around and ask around
about lonely people whose hearts were in bad shape.
They made it their business
to be on the lookout
for opportunities to wright some hearts,
and when they found the right situation,
they would go around
with their portable stereo tape deck
and, rather than use it as a boom box
and turning the volume up to full blast to drive people crazy
all over a six block radius,
they would spend an hour or two
playing the favorite music for the people
whose hearts were in bad shape,
all those lonely people
who only needed a little music in their lives.
They carried three carrying cases full of tapes
and, if they were old people they went to visit,
they would ask,
"Would you like to hear,
'Let Me Call You Sweetheart'
or 'Alexander's Ragtime Band'?"
and if the old people said, "Yes,"
they'd just pop the tape in and play it,
even playing it 2 or 4 or 10 times
if that's what the person wanted to hear.
And if they went to see some baby boomers
who were having a hard time at the moment,
they remembered to pack a lot of Oldies But Goodies
with Elvis at the top of the list,
and the Everly Brothers and Bill Haley and the Comets,
and from what Ilana, Reena and Shosh tell me,
as soon as "You Ain't Nuthin' But a Hound Dog"
or "Rock Around the Clock"

blasted the air and made it rattle and roll
everyone's face lit up.
There were even a number of recorded incidents
of formerly gloomy people who were pushing 50
who got up to do a jitterbug
before they remembered they were supposed to be sad.
(One or two managed a fairly respectable Twist,
and a particularly happy listener went from the Cha-Cha-Cha
to some other wild whirl around the room
in a crazy dance whose name I forgot.)
And they of course kept in stock
a goodly number of mushy songs for teen-agers,
all slow numbers,
every one of them extremely gooey,
and The Beatles and The Rolling Stones
as old standbys
and a few dozen of the classic nursery rhymes tapes
and tapes of Peter, Paul, and Mary singing kiddie songs
for kiddies who were sad
and who should never be sad.
In fact,
if you look at record books,
you'll see that Ilana, Reena and Shosh
had the biggest collection of Tikun Olam tapes
in all of Louisville
and probably the entire state of Kentucky.

In General, Tikun Olamniks Can Do It Better In Pairs, Triplets, Quads, Quints, And Larger Groups

If you have to fix the handlebars on a bike,
obviously it is best if two people do it:
one to hold the bike real steady
and the other to use the screwdriver and wrenches
to straighten the handlebars.
It makes sense.
I mean, think of the electric company.
Would they ever try to fix wires up on those big poles

with only one person on the job?
They really do need wire-fixer high up in the cherrypicker
and a sorter-and-organizer down below to sort and organize
and send up the right materials
to get the juice flowing again
to all the houses in the neighborhood.
When the repavers have to repave a strip of road,
besides the person sitting on the steamroller,
there had better be a few flagpersons out there
to slow the traffic down.
The steamroller driver just couldn't do it alone,
and neither could the people from the fire department
without the crew from the rescue squad being there.
And if there's twenty acres of land
that were flooded in a flood
and the town needed to plant a new grove of
sycamores and birches or spruces or firs,
one person doing all that replanting
just wouldn't be enough.
And if you think the chef —
either at a fancy-schmancy restaurant
or at a shelter
or at a family-style Mom and Pop wholesome
down home clean place for the family place
in the medium price range
or one of those with the giant salad bars
with nine types of dressings
including Low-Fat French, Thousand Island, and Ranch
in the bargain range —
if you think the chef can do it
without the celery-and-carrot-and-broccoli chopper
and the bean soaker
and the pie crust pincher
who makes that nice ring around the edges of the crust
of the lemon meringue or Boston cream pie,
if you think he or she can do it alone,
you'll have to rethink how things work
in this world.
And how would it be
if *The Chicago Sun-Times* or *The Miami Herald*
sent out a reporter to cover The Special Olympics

but didn't send a photographer?
Do you think that's the best way
to tell people about such a fabulous news story?
And just try to find me one sane lion surgeon
who has to work on a lion who's been roaring
at the top of his lungs for three days straight
because he has a thorn in his paw —
try to find me even one
who's willing to try the surgery
without a trusty anesthesiologist
right there beside him
to make absolutely, positively sure
the lion is very much asleep.
Ha, not a chance!
He'd have to be totally out of his mind
to try that little bit of worldwrighting
all by himself.
Couldn't do it. He just couldn't do it.
He'd have to be what they call in Yiddish
"Gantz Meshuggeh"
which roughly means "100% out of his gourd".

Barnraising, The Classic Case Of How a Tikun Olam Gang (Or What I Like to Call "The Chevra") Does Their Thing in a Big Way Between Sunrise and Sunset

I think barnraising is the best example I can think of
for getting the Tikun Olam Gang together.
If, somewhere where Amish people live,
someone needs a barn,
well, plain and simple,
their Tikun Olam Gang comes out in full force at dawn
and starts to build,
and by the time the sun sets
there's a brand spanking new barn standing there
where yesterday there was
nothing but a piece of empty land.
Can you beat that for worldwrighting?

And those are just a few examples
of how members of
The International Sisterhood and Brotherhood
of Heartwrights and Worldwrights
can do that much more
if they get together
and share their time and energy and IQ and talents
for Tikun Olam.
I am sure I, or you, or anyone
could make a list 100 times as long
if we just took the time to think about it,
and, after we think about it,
do something about it.
Of course.

T.O.U.

Learning a Skill

If you want to be a carpenter
and haven't got the vaguest idea
how to use a plane or buzz saw,
it's best to spend time learning from someone
who's good with planes and buzz saws
and who's been using them for years.
The same goes for future plumbers.
The pros can teach you everything you need to know
about water pressure and joints and pipes
and which kind of iron is best
for what kind of system,
and what kind of lead is just not good for anyone,
and, as for computers,
to become a whiz at Windows and Word and Excel,
if you don't sign up for a good stretch of time
with someone who likes to spend 16 hours a day
in front of a screen,
you're just going to keep slogging along
with little hope of ever designing
The Ultimate Fuel Injection System for a Jaguar
or making beautiful Mother's Day cards for Dear Old Mom.
Now some of them might look like geeks or dweebs,
but they are still experts,
and they really know their stuff,
so there's no good reason to be afraid to try it.

A Special Case: Concert Bassooning

If you want to learn music
and want to be good enough
and think you have the talent
to be a concert cellist, bassoonist, or French horner,
sooner or later
you have to study with a maestro or maestra
cellist, bassoonist, or French horner.

Doctor, Lawyer, Businessperson

If you want to be a doctor,
you need medical school,
a lawyer, law school,
a business honcha or honcho, business school.

College

And don't get me wrong,
all of those things help
when it comes to Tikun Olam.
And don't get me wrong,
I think very highly of Yale
and the University of Alaska, Fairbanks,
and Reed College in Portland, OR,
and all those California schools
with their alphabet abbreviations:
UCLA, UCD (Davis), UCSB (Santa Barbara),
UCSC (Santa Cruz), and UCSD (San Diego),
just to name a few.

T.O.U.

But what we're looking for is training
that takes everything else we learn
and pours it into fixing up the world,
like, for just one example, in one of the new catalogues
the listing for a Major in Dreamwrighting
that trains the students
in the human art of teaching people
to dream at all
and how to dream the best of all dreams
and how to rebuild shattered dreams they once had
but may have forgotten
because Life got tough for a few years
and their dreams got dragged down
and lost in the shuffle of just getting by.
Those are the kinds of things
you learn at T.O.U.,
Tikun Olam University.

What T.O.U. Offers Concerning Microwaves, Plymouths, And $16 Elbow Braces

Like,
say you just finished a massive minicourse elective
in "Applied Household Appliance Repair"
because you needed a break
from "5th and 6th Dimensional Geometry"
and "Swamp Flora and Fauna in the Mississippi Delta:
A Field Study"
and "The Interactivity of Muons and Pi Mesons"
(which by themselves would be quite a heavy load to carry
in one semester,
and all three at once, capable of twisting many a good mind
into terrible shapes)
and, just for fun,
and because you're good at it,
you get an A or A-
and are now able to take apart a vacuum cleaner
or espresso machine or one of those newfangled breadmakers
that look like they have cousins on Jupiter or beyond.
Say you are at the top of the class
and the other students are envious of your skill.
Maybe you still wouldn't know
what a wonderful thing it would be
to get microwave ovens to people who are blind
because they are easy to use and because they are safe,
and because it is very easy to put braille numbers and letters
up on the keyboard
to make it easy for them to read with their fingers.
So you would only be halfway there,
"there" being in the real world of Tikun Olam.
And if you decided second semester to take "Car Repair 101"
three times a week in the afternoons
to keep your sanity
after three times a week in the morning of
"Ontological and Existential Breakthroughs
in the Very, Very Early Writings of Kirkegaard",
you might be able to change fan belts on your own
and plug or replace a muffler with the best of them,

After the Rain

but you might not think,
"Wouldn't it be just fine
to make sure blind people had a car?"
for two good reasons, at least:
(a) because everyone else on the block has one
and they might be embarrassed if they didn't,
and (b) others could drive them to work or a concert
or a picnic in the park
if everyone else's other cars were being used
by their teen-age daughters and sons
to go to The Big Game.
You might even be the great genius in engineering,
astonishing your professors
with your command of stress points on bridges
and vectors and calculus and electromagnetism,
and when it comes down to it,
with your diploma in hand
and your Mom and Dad sitting way down there
right in the middle of the 97th row of the audience
making a video record
to show your grandchildren some day,
you still might not have thought to do something like
figuring out how to make an elbow brace
for someone whose elbow doesn't work just right
and who really needs one,
and you could have done your Senior Project on it
and might have come up with a design that costs only $16
and, just for fun, at the same time
could have sent around to all the Elbow Brace Manufacturers
in the country or the world
who might have sent back estimates for $80,000.
And I didn't make those up
because I know the man who knew about microwaves and cars
for his blind friends
and I read the article on elbow braces with my own eyes
and I said to myself,
"Now who in the world would have thought of such things?"
and I knew the answer was,
"Well, for the microwaves and the Plymouths,
just about anyone,
and for the elbow brace,

After the Rain

just about anyone who learned some engineering
and had a chance to take all that genius
and put it to some extra good."
And to wrap it up:
think of all the worldwrighting that could be done
with the $79,984 left over
from not spending $80,000
on the other
probably-also-very-nice-but-way-overpriced elbow brace.

The T.O.U. Basic Math Requirement

And let's say
while we are thinking about the microwaves and Plymouths
and that bargain-priced elbow brace,
let's say
at this moment there are 27,645
broken and breaking pieces in this world,
of which 21,476 are easily and immediately fixable.
Then let's get down to easily and immediately fixing
the 21,476 easily and immediately fixable pieces,
which leaves only 6,169 tougher ones,
of which 5,945 of them can be solved
by Nobel Prize Quality Tikun Olamniks
who are probably working on them right now
and will solve them very soon or soon,
which leaves us with only 224
incredibly difficult and long-term pieces to fix
of which I am sure the delegates to
The Annual International Conference
of Worldwrights, Heartwrights, and Tikun Olamniks
will solve 183 of them with their minds, hearts, souls, and hands
and Mitzvah money
which specialists in finding Mitzvah money often can find
(though sometimes they are a little short)
which leaves us with only
41 nearly impossible bits of fixing
to do.
Some people would say it would take a miracle to get them done,
but any good Worldwright knows
that miracles happen more often than regular people think.

More About T.O.U.
And Two Other Very Fine Places
To Get This Kind of Education

So you see,
for this kind of education,
may I suggest three places to study,
all of them in America's Heartland:
Worldwright College
on the outskirts of Hot Springs, SD,
just about an hour South of Rapid City,
(with other branches all around the state),
or Heartwright Tech
in Maxwell, NE, just East of North Platte,
(which has satellite campuses over the border
in Cedar Rapids, Des Moines, and Waterloo, IA,
with another opening soon in Grand Island, back in NE),
and, of course, the best place of all —
T.O.U., Tikun Olam University.
And though T,O.U.'s main campus
is located in Sioux City —
you may have guessed...
it offers courses everywhere you can think of.
I particularly like their motto:

Chevra
Post Regens
Sol et Caelestis Arcus
Semper

at least, that's the best I can remember it,
though my Latin grammar is weak
after so many years away from my textbooks.
As best as I can translate it, it means:

Chevra!
After the Rain,
Sun and the Rainbow.
Always.

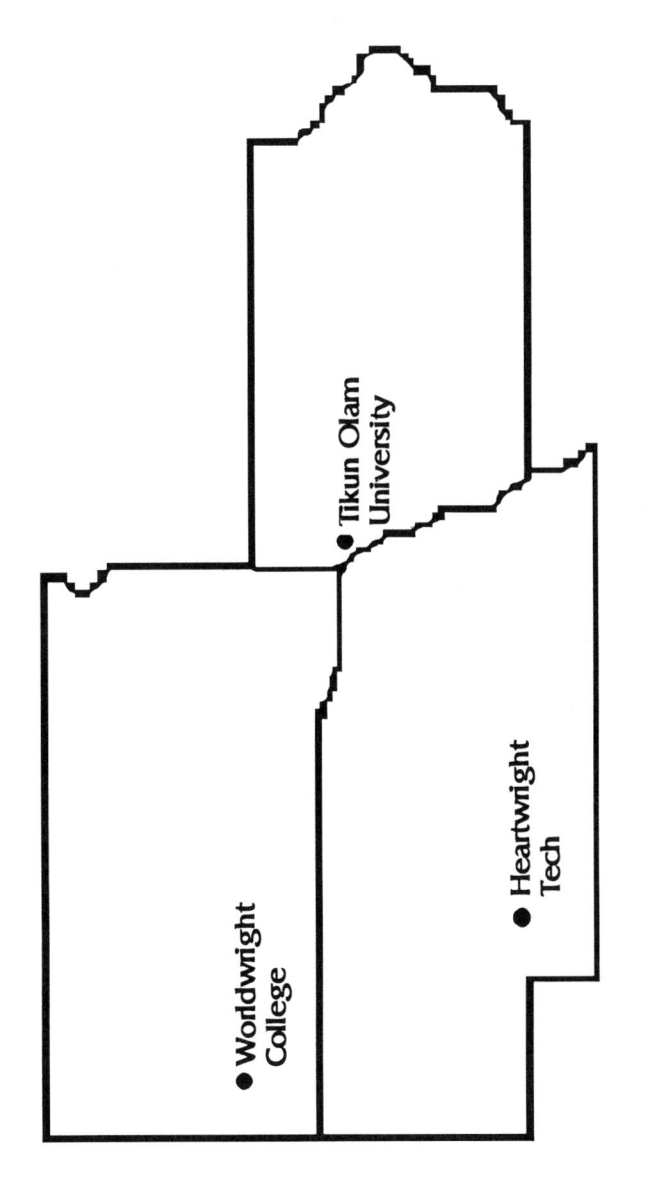

The Mitzvah Schools

- Tikun Olam University
- Worldwright College
- Heartwright Tech

After the Rain

And to tell you the truth,
T.O.U. isn't really an institution.
It's wherever good people and goodhearted people
and world-handy people
are to be found.
They are the best teachers and professors
and whenever you work with them,
they are teaching and you are learning.
They know how to take everything
anybody ever learned in books
and put it into Tikun Olam action.
They know heartwrighting and worldwrighting
better than anyone
and they are everywhere.
All you have to do is find one of them
and say, "Here I am.
Teach me what to do with what I've got,"
and you can be sure they will take it from there,
and before long, and without a doubt,
you, yourself, will become
a great heartwright or worldwright
and can keep the cycle going
as you teach others
how to fix breaking hearts
and repair the broken world.

Names and Titles for Yourself
If You Want to Make Up
A Little Business Card,
Some Stationery, And a T-Shirt

Making a Title

First you need your name.
Then you need some words to describe how good you are at fixing things
like super, awesome, sensational, radical, incredible,
astonishing, supreme, most excellent, high-powered,
wowie, zowie, wowie zowie,
or anything else that might appeal to your own taste.
Then you need fixing words,
like if you use paste to fix things up, "Paster",
or Crayons, "Crayonist".
You can even use a lot of the "re" words
if that will get you rolling.

Putting Them Together

When you put them all together,
You might come up with things like:
Renana the Radical Redoer
if your best way of fixing things is to redo them.
Then there's Oren the Outstanding Overhauler,
if you specialize in Tikun Olam overhauling,
or if you have decided to be an expert
in using magic to cheer up a down-and-out heart,
you might put on your stationery
Big Mike the Marvelous Mitzvah Magician,
and if are a terrific tinkerer
and use that great talent for tinkering
to fix up some of hearts that are hurting
as often as you might have a chance,
you could become
Talya the Terrific Tikun Olam Tinkerer with Tools,

After the Rain

or Fran the Fantastic Fiddler-Around
if it happens that you do your best repair work
after you have fiddled around a little
so you can find the best possible way to fix
that part of the world that is
right in front of you at that moment
that needs your attention...
right then
and not a single minute later.

Just like others have titles like
Dr. or DDS or PhD or Prof.
you now have your own:
Shimon the Supreme Reshaper,
Willy the World Champion Worldwright,
or Rakefet the Radical Reweaver of Unraveling Hearts.
And just like MSW, Lt. Col. and Esq.
tell us something about the person,
so, too, we know a lot about
Rachel and Reuven when we read their titles:
Reuven the Remarkable Reconditioner of
Worn-out Hearts
and Rachel the Irresistibly Outrageous Restorer
of Run-down Worlds, Class A.

Keeping Them In Your Drawer

But you won't want to hand out these cards
or use this stationery for letters
because it's best not to brag about
your Tikun Olam work.
Fixing up the world is good to do
because it's a Mitzvah
and the right thing to do
and it makes the world a better place
for every person on earth
not to mention the oak trees and ponderosas
and monarch butterflies
and the millions of red, pink, and gray snapper
in the Seven Seas.
Still, you can keep the stationery in your drawer

After the Rain

and use one or two of the cards maybe as a bookmark
so you can look at them once in a while
to remind yourself that it might be time
to do a little more Worldwrighting or Heartwrighting
on that particular day.

The Tikun Olam T-Shirt

Also,
getting a big T-shirt in bright orange and screaming blue
that says "Miriam the Magnificent Fixer-Upper"
might not be a great idea
because you don't want to brag.
But it is perfectly all right to dream about
a T-shirt like that.
You can design it any way you want in your imagination,
with medium-length sleeves or sequins
and a clawhammer
and something-with-three-or-four-good-sized-prongs
on the back,
whatever your favorite Tikun Olam tools are,
maybe even a sphyg
or on the back a woofer and a tweeter
and on the front
a big heart.
You can decide best of all
because it's your own private imaginary Tikun Olam T-shirt.
And if you really wanted to,
I suppose you could make a real one,
and it would be OK to wear it around the house
or in the back yard if the family is having
a 4th of July cook-out with
chicken franks, turkeyburgers, corn, salad,
cole slaw, fries, and, of course, watermelon
so juicy you would have to be careful
not to drip any juice on your Tikun Olam T-shirt.
Yes, that would be all right.
No one would think you were bragging
if you just wore it around the house
among family and friends.

What Began With A Frammis

This whole thing began because
I was worried about a slipped frammis
which I couldn't find anywhere,
not in the brake shoes, not under the spare tire,
not even hiding in the back of the glove compartment
behind the Owner's Manual for my Dodge.
Now see where it has taken me and you.
I read all kinds of books
and looked at all kinds of charts and diagrams,
but still couldn't find the frammis
without the help of my mechanic.
Nevertheless, all along I knew
someone out there knew where it was
and, if it broke or slipped off its joint or gasket,
he or she would know just how to fix it, and,
maybe with a little luck, when I found that person,
he or she would show me where it was,
tell me what was wrong with it,
and show me how to fix it myself
so I wouldn't have to panic ever again
if it slipped off its belt or broke.

The same goes for Tikun Olam.
The Good People everywhere
will teach anyone who wants to know
how to fix all things breaking and broken in this world —
including hearts and dreams —
and along the way we will learn such things as
why we are here
and what we are supposed to be doing
with our hands and minds and souls and our time.
That way, we can hope to find out why
we were given a human heart,
and that way, we can hope to know
the hearts of other human beings.
and the heart of the world.

DANNY SIEGEL is a free-lance author, poet, and lecturer who resides in Rockville, Maryland, when not on his speaking tours or in Israel distributing Tzedakah monies.

For more than a decade, he has concentrated most of his writings on Tzedakah, attempting to focus the public's attention on the deeds of loving-kindness. *Mitzvahs*, published in 1990, was the latest in this essay series. His previous works on Tzedakah: *Munbaz II and Other Mitzvah Heroes, Gym Shoes and Irises, Books One and Two*, have become the standard guideline text for personalized tzedakah.

His publication of *Family Reunion: Making Peace in the Jewish Community*, addressed the painful subject of disunity and polarization, making an attempt to sows the seeds of harmony.

The Meadow Beyond The Meadow, published in 1991, was Danny's sixth book of poetic writings, first begun in 1969 with the publication of *Soulstoned*, a collector's item now out of print. Following on the heels on *Meadow's* remarkable success, Danny created *A Hearing Heart*.

Siegel is a popular lecturer at synagogues, Jewish federations, community centers, conventions, and retreats, where he teaches Tzedakah and Jewish values and recites from his works. His books and talks have received considerable acclaim throughout the entire North American Jewish community.

BOOKS BY DANNY SIEGEL

Mitzvahs	1980 -	ANGELS*
	1982 -	GYM SHOES AND IRISES* (Personalized Tzedakah)
	1987 -	GYM SHOES AND IRISES - BOOK TWO*
	1988 -	MUNBAZ II AND OTHER MITZVAH HEROES
	1989 -	FAMILY REUNION: Making Peace in the Jewish Community
	1990 -	MITZVAHS
	1993 -	AFTER THE RAIN: The Book of Mitzvah Power for Adults and Teens
Children's Stories	1993 -	TELL ME A MITZVAH *(Published by Kar-Ben Copies)*
Humor	1982 -	THE UNORTHODOX BOOK OF JEWISH RECORDS AND LISTS (With Allan Gould)
Poetry	1969 -	SOULSTONED*
	1976 -	AND GOD BRAIDED EVE'S HAIR*
	1978 -	BETWEEN DUST AND DANCE*
	1980 -	NINE ENTERED PARADISE ALIVE*
	1983 -	UNLOCKED DOORS (An Anthology)
	1985 -	THE GARDEN: Where Wolves and Lions Do No Harm to the Sheep and the Deer
	1985 -	THE LORD IS A WHISPER AT MIDNIGHT (Psalms and Prayers)
	1986 -	BEFORE OUR VERY EYES Readings for a Journey Through Israel
	1991 -	THE MEADOW BEYOND THE MEADOW
	1992 -	A HEARING HEART
Midrash and Halachah	1983 -	WHERE HEAVEN AND EARTH TOUCH (Book One)*
	1984 -	WHERE HEAVEN AND EARTH TOUCH (Book Two)*
	1985 -	WHERE HEAVEN AND EARTH TOUCH (Book Three)*
	1985 -	WHERE HEAVEN AND EARTH TOUCH SOURCE BOOK (Selected Hebrew and Aramaic Sources)
	1988 -	WHERE HEAVEN AND EARTH TOUCH (Combined Volumes: Book One, Two and Three)
	1989 -	WHERE HEA (Combi

*Out of print